For the Blood and the Buckle

American Rodeo
Born of the Open Range

By Jim Bartlett

Printed in the United States of America

First Edition 2023

ISBN 978-1-7353222-6-1

Carentan Media Group

Carentanmedia@proton.me

In Memory of Lane Frost

1963 – 1989

A champion bull rider, Lane was fatally injured at the 1989 Frontier Days rodeo in Cheyenne, WY.

His death was the catalyst for introduction of protective equipment now mandatory on the bull riding circuit.

He was 25.

So tip your hat to the cowboy every once in a while,
And take time to remember that cowboy's smile.
A little part of every heart of every rodeo fan,
Died there in the rain and the mud in July in Cheyenne.
Aaron Watson, July in Cheyenne.

How I come by this

I guess cattle, rodeo, the frontier, it always ran in my blood. Back in the day my grandfather, Clarence "Skipper" Bartlett, had a falling out with a stepfather. He went to the neighbor's house for refuge, but the neighbor told him that he couldn't stay long term. But the neighbor had an idea. There was a friend out in Montana, and he felt the boy to go see the west before it was gone. This was in Topsham, Maine in 1911. Clarence was 16.

So a ticket was bought and a week or so later the young man debarked onto the platform in Billings, Montana. Seeing a stray youth standing there, and noticing the strange accent, the station master inquired as to why. Clarence told him the story but was met with the disappointing news that the neighbor's friend had died some time back. The station master, however, knew someone who would take him in. This turned out to be a hog farmer outside of town who took him on as an indentured servant of sorts. This went on for some months.

Fortunately for Clarence the family was in town one day, and there was a cattle drive in town. The boy started talking with some of the cowboys, who noticed his funny, Maine accent and inquired as to how he came to Montana. Upon hearing his tale of woe, they determined to rescue him from the hog farm life. Passing the hat, they collected $20 and "purchased" him from the farmer.

And thus began his life on the Double D Ranch. The life of a real cowboy: tending horses, moving cows, fixing fences, roping calves, branding, and in the off time, trick riding, broncs, bulls, and bulldogging. I mean, what else was there to do, out in the middle of nowhere somewhere near Glendive, Montana in 1911?

He stayed out there until the outbreak of WW1, when he joined the U.S. Cavalry, serving in C Troop of the 12th. He brought with him all the skills he had learned in Montana, becoming a member of the trick riding team. He returned to Maine and established a school of equitation in the Naples region where all of this was passed onto my father. He was known for riding two horses Roman style down the causeway between Long Lake and Brandy Pond. Dad became a trick rider of note himself and spent the rest of his life caring for horses as an equine vet.

So, yea, I guess that's where it comes from.

Brimstone and Barbed Wire Fences

My grasp of why I find this so endearing is ethereal at best. It's all kind of mish mashed together into this brew of nostalgia, hopeless romance, smells, grit, and a deep and abiding respect for the sheer toughness of everyone and everything associated with the working of cattle...which is where rodeo comes from. It was born in the American West. Beautiful and deadly all in one, even today. It defined us as a people.

Once you've drunk deeply of it, there's really no going back. It's vast, and the sky is endless. It's you versus the elements and anything else it wants to throw at you. Like the winters of my native New England, it takes a toughness to ride it out. No wonder the official pastime of this place involves hoisting yourself onto large animals that do not want you doing that, who violently try to eject you. People get legitimately hurt doing this. Some die. It's a reflection of just trying to live in the west.

It's an embodiment of a people. The grit required to tend livestock day after day, in any weather, brings a humbleness that makes them reserved, but approachable at the same time. They're the kind of people you want as a neighbor if something goes sideways...like a blizzard, a tornado, or really any other problem. Frontier people. You survive by pulling together and facing whatever gets thrown at you. That's the cultural baseline and rodeo is the national sport that grew out of that legacy.

ABC BODY SHOP
31

RideNow

POLARIS
Capri

AT

Broncs: Because you need horses to move cows.

Perhaps the foundational event in rodeo is bronc riding. It emerged from the need to break horses to saddle as you're not going to move cows on foot. They're not necessarily born wanting you on top of them, so sooner or later man and horse must come to an arrangement. Even with the most gentle handed approach, most will try to get the human off at least once in the beginning.

Every ranch has a ring where this arrangement is reached. Some would be reached quickly, some slowly, and some not at all. The horses in the latter category were known (and still are) as "rank." The seriously rank ones go down in legend as "The one's that can't be rode." In some cases their memories have outlived the cowboys who tried. Old Red and The Brute are but two Marty Robbins immortalized. And then there's Old Steamboat or Deadman. Depending on who you ask, they're the horses featured on the Wyoming State symbol of the bucking cowboy. Which one is still hotly debated to this day. A couple of horses. They still argue about this...

Back in the day they were just ornery horses on a ranch that didn't take to the saddle and of course became the focus of "I bet you can't" events. Today they are specialized equine athletes, selective bred for the purpose, and scored as closely as the riders. They accumulate points and there are substantial payouts, as well as a shot at bucking stock bronc of the year for the best of them.

DILLON
Q929

037
OCALA

Marion County
SOUTHEAS
SOUTHEASTERN

NOW HIR
eview
Hospital

Roping

The second tie-in to actual ranch work are the roping events. It's a key part of managing the springtime workload. Cows have to be corralled, roped, branded, vax'd, neutered if they're a steer, and then released. Rope work and special horses trained for this are necessary.

This is where the real grit has to kick in. When you have a herd of several hundred cattle it turns into a long day. They have to be sorted, with special "cutting" horses that push individual cows out of the herd, which is something a herd animal doesn't want to do (and there's a whole separate sport devoted to those horses). Then the calves have to be roped, brought down, tagged, and given their shots. These are animals that already weigh a couple hundred pounds. They don't want any part of any of this. This is rough work. It also must happen during a certain window, so weather is whatever it's going to be. In places like Montana or Wyoming in the early spring, that can be pretty miserable. If there's a certain romance around riding the open range through summer into fall, the price of entry is the spring round up.

Of course, this work naturally found its way into rodeo. There's calf, or "Tie down" roping, which involves and single rider who ropes and then ties the calf up as you would working stock. There's team roping, which involves two riders, an older steer, and the objective is to lasso them front and back. And then there's breakaway roping, which is largely a women's event. They rope the calf but don't do the whole tie down thing as the lasso is held by a string and breaks away when the cow takes up the slack. All of these are timed events. Top ropers are hitting times in the single and low double digits

Roping is the most inclusive of all rodeo events. Anyone with a decent throw and a good horse can participate. They start young. You see kids as young as 5 or 6 lassoing anything they can get a rope around. A retired rope in the hands of a ranch kid is the western equivalent of a soccer ball in other parts of the world.

For those concerned about the cows. There are rules, lots of rules and even protective head gear for the steers. There's vets and animal EMS on site. These are valuable animals. People take care of them.

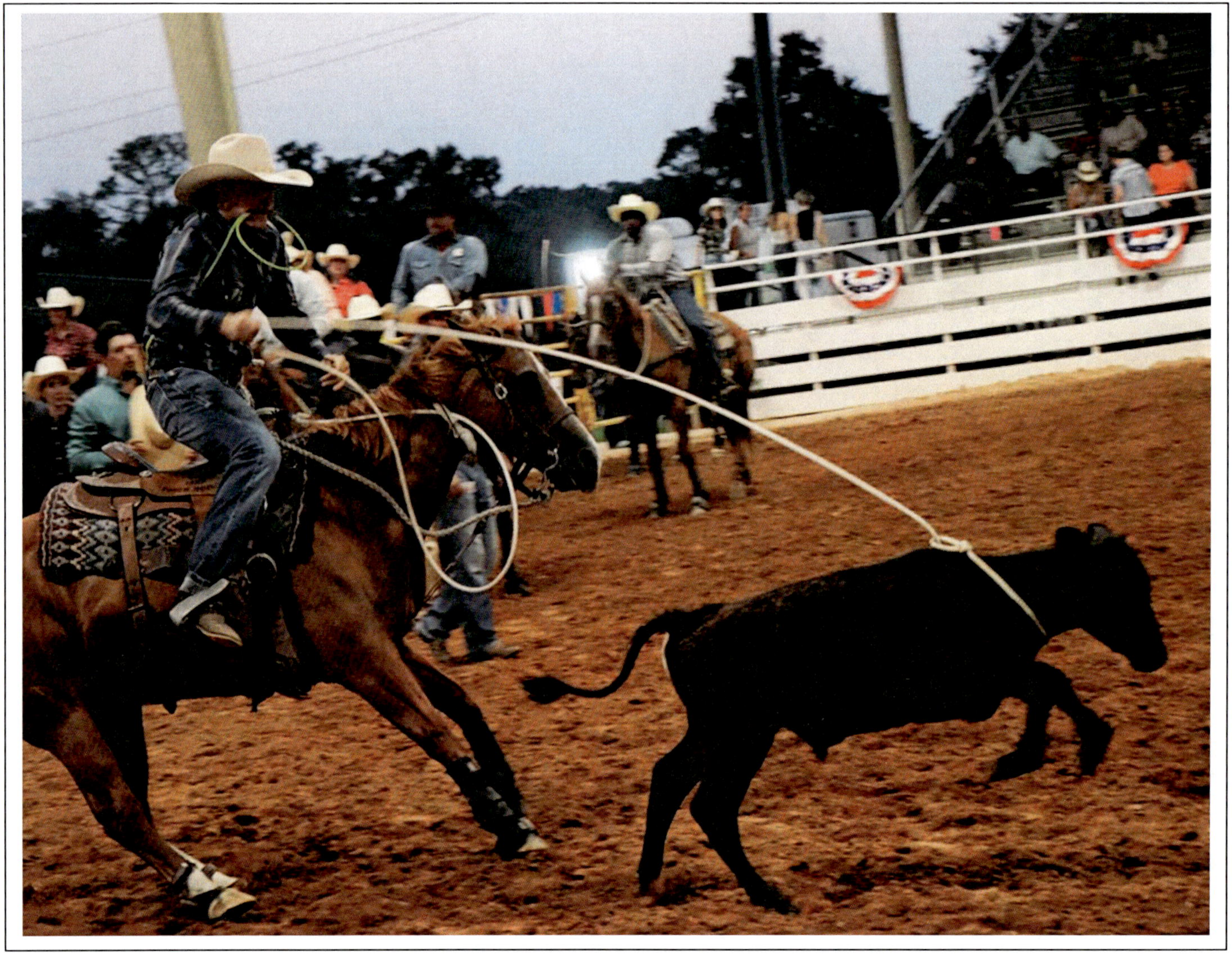

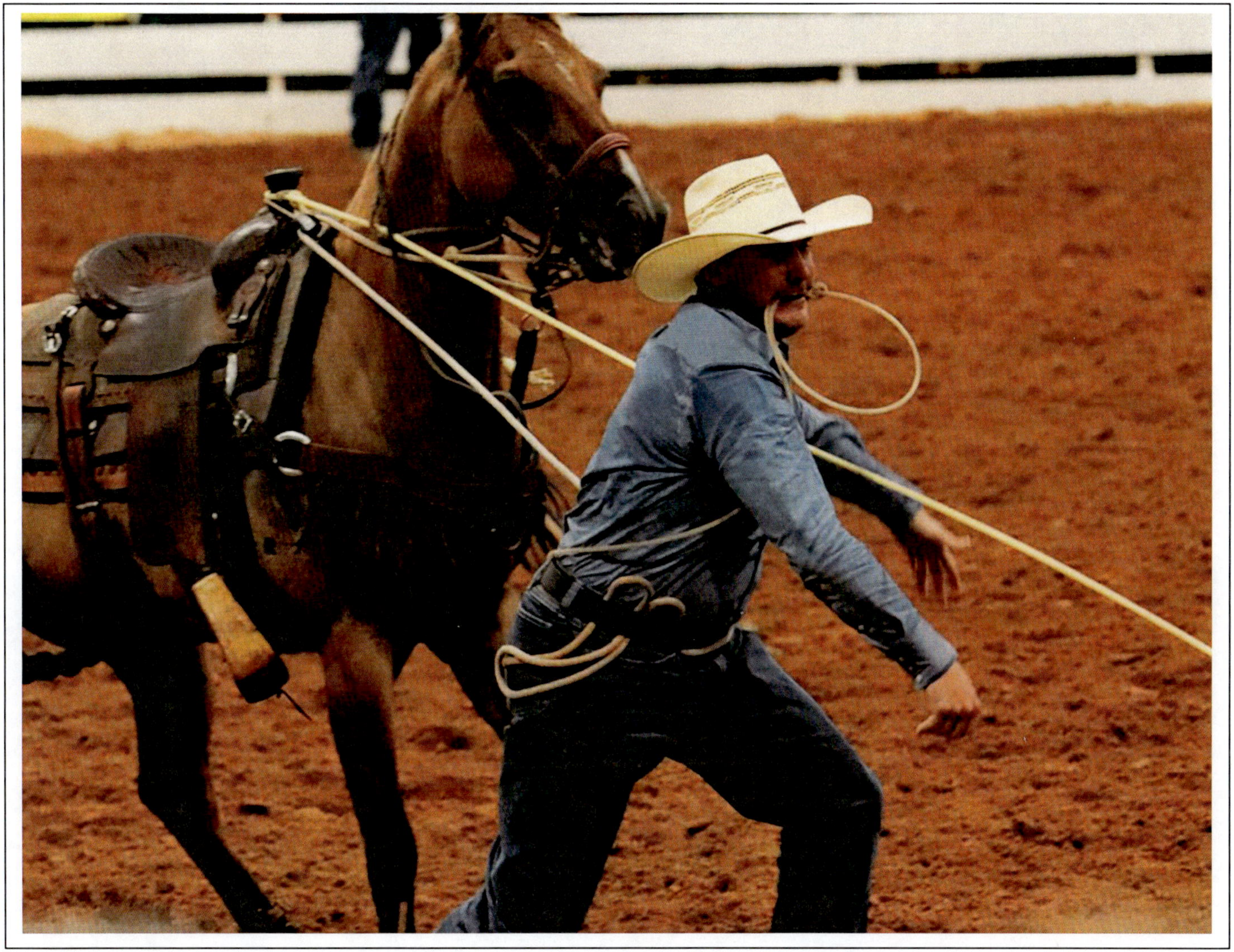

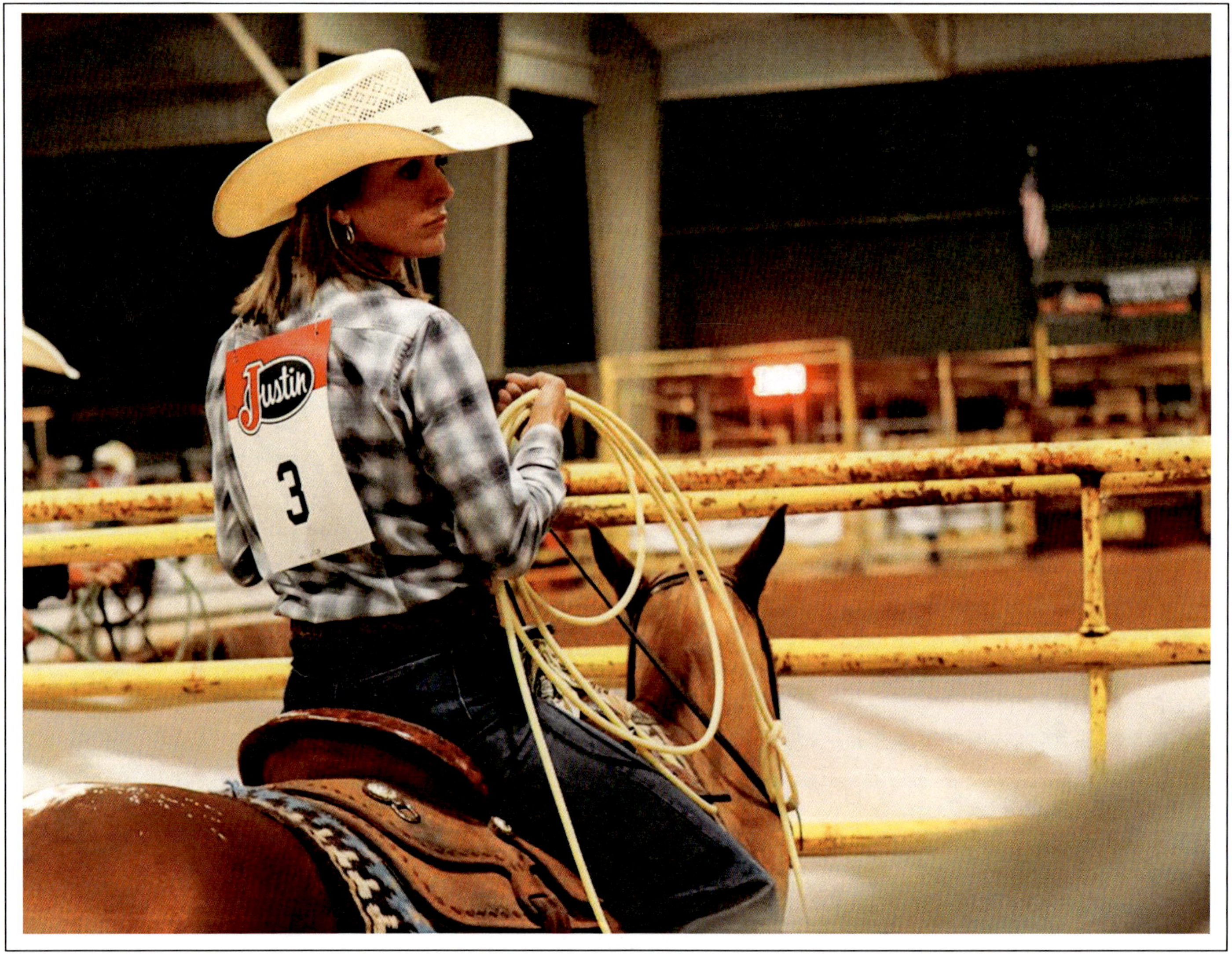
Justin
3

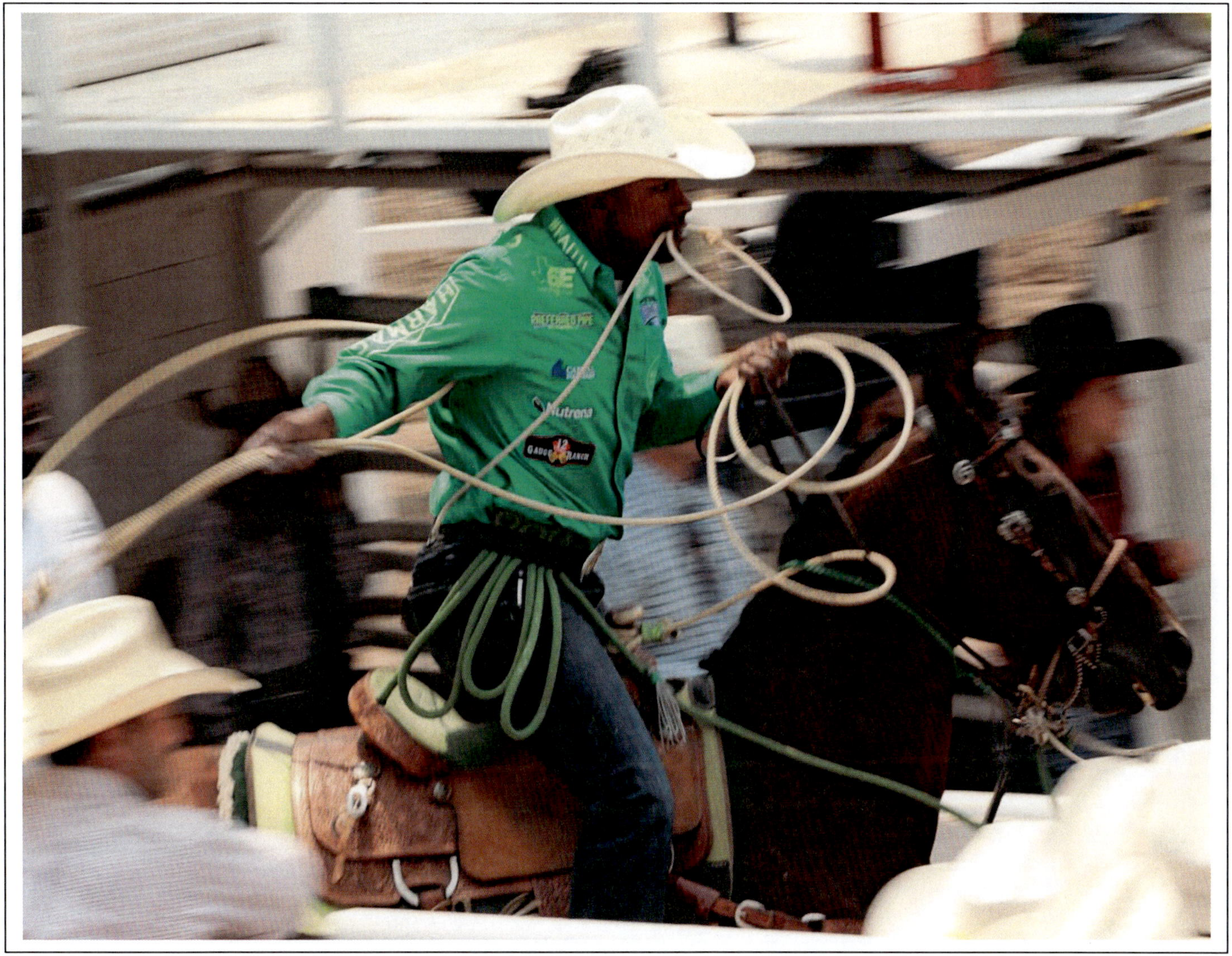
PREFERRED PIPE
Nutrena

Priefer
Priefer

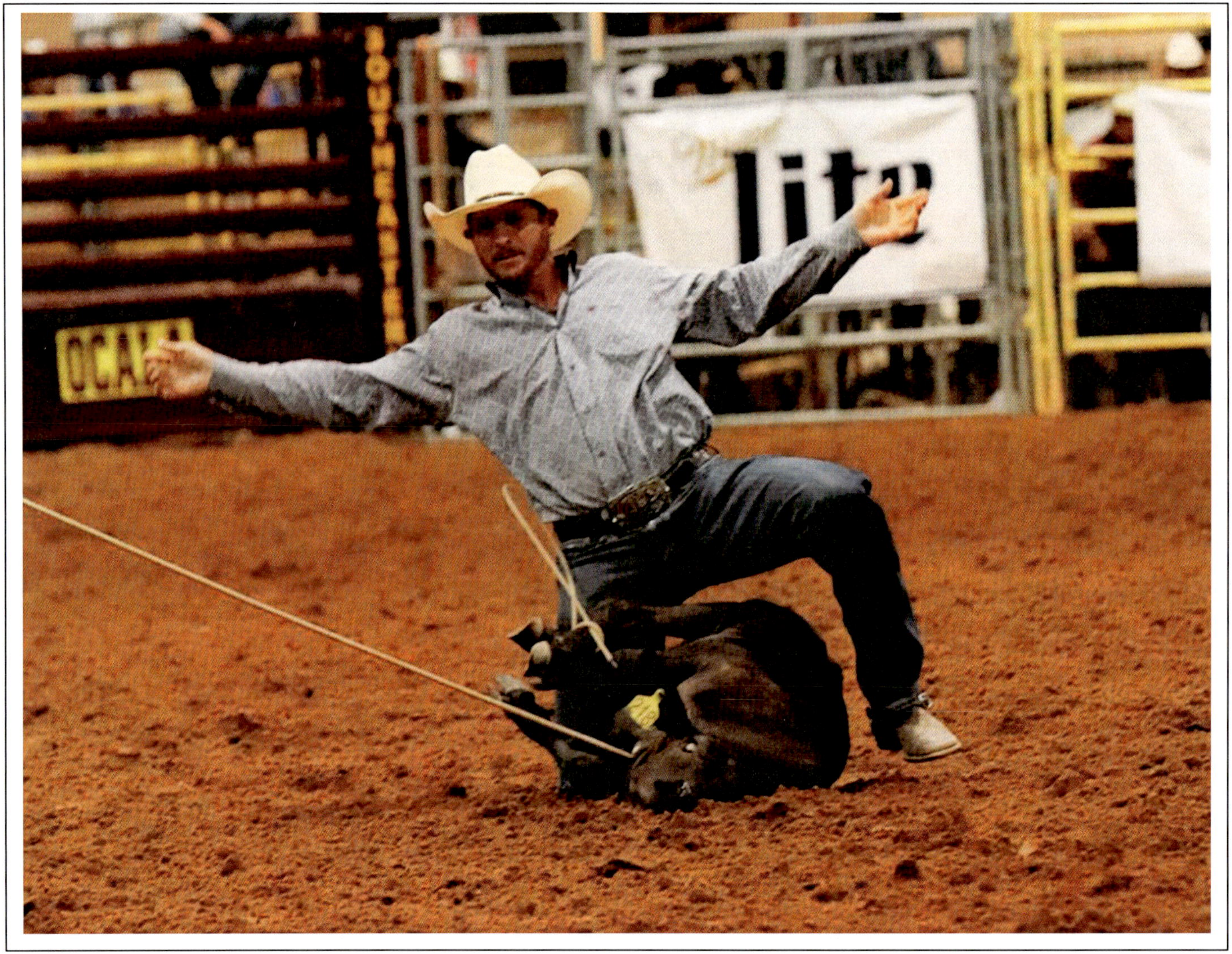
lite

Bulldogging

Credit for the public event of bulldogging goes to Bill Picket in the 1890s who featured it as part of his Wild West show. I cannot imagine, however, that there wasn't some "I'm bored, let's see if we can wrestle this steer to the ground" with an assist from "I bet you cain't," mixed in from over on the ranch side. Think about it. Young men, bored, with egos, on some ranch in the middle of nowhere. No way did Bill just come up with this.

Today its known as Steer Wrestling and regardless of where it really came from, it's a staple of modern rodeo.

It's simple enough in concept. Ride your horse alongside the running steer, jump onto him, grab him around the horns and drag him to the ground. Easy, right?

To keep things lined up, there's a second rider that runs alongside so the steer will stay in a straight line. Love ya brothers, but you're always getting in the frame.

DILLON

SOUTHEASTE
NOW
FOR ALL POSITI
LEGACY LAWN &

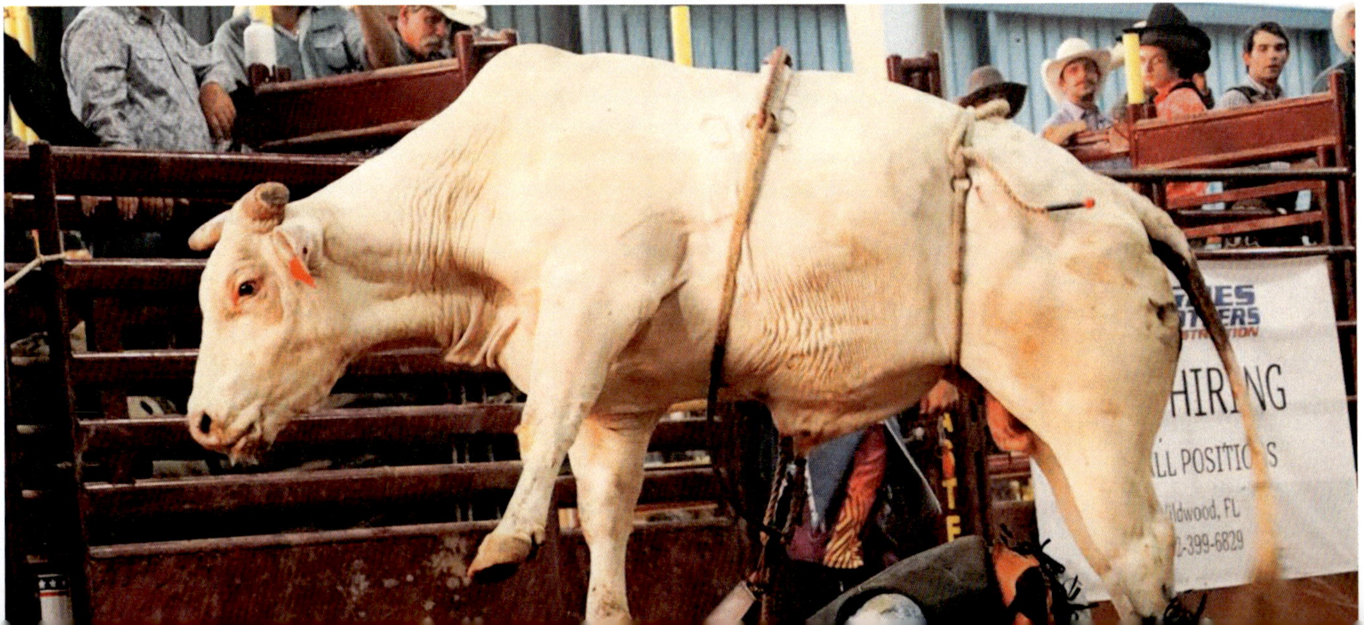
HIRING

SOUTHE
LEGACY LAWN
GHES

Rank Bulls

This is where rodeo gets deadly serious. Of all the events in this arena, bull riding is by far the most dangerous. People die, literally. It's also the most lucrative. The saying "He's a million dollar bull rider," which refers to annual winnings, speaks to this. It's also the most international of all the events, with riders from places like Brazil taking more than a few national championships.

The history of bull riding, as much as we know, goes back to Minoan times. Makes sense, being one of those things that lends itself to young men proving a point in front of their friends and pretty girls. In our modern time it dates back to when America absorbed Spanish holdings in the west, where it had been a staple of the collective Mexican ranch events known as Charreada.

The bucking stock bulls, like their equine counterparts, are

RING
ITIONS
SOUTH

Rodeo
451
352-732-7577

RCH at TR
10-6067.
NW 100 Avenue

SOUTHSIDE
RODEO

ALL POSITIONS
OCALA, FL

BUTLER
CINCH

Rodeo Roadies

Without rodeo staff who work for the companies who produce these events, there would be no rodeo. Behind the scenes there's a lot of moving pieces. Venues must be maintained, infrastructures for the care of animals must be provided for, entries and rankings tracked and reported up the organizational chains, etc, etc.

The companies that put on these events range from small, family owned outfits at the local level to large, multi-million dollar syndicates that throw the big ones like the national finals in Vegas. That's the stuff you don't see.

In the ring you have the presenters who MC the show, the wranglers who manage the stock, and the bullfighters who go head to head with the bulls as part of the safety net for downed bull riders. NFL running backs can't hold a candle to those guys in the agility department.

Some of the folks come in for an event or two locally, but others spend the season on the road, just as the contestants do. Like the folks who travel with the fair / carnival circuit, but a bit tamer.

Without them there would be no rodeo.

RODEO
Wrangler

PRORODEO
PRCA
MONTANA

AT
AT

OCALA

INSURANCE
671-3332
Community Since 2004

Rodeo People

Rodeo people come in every variety. I've met everyone from oil & gas big wigs to the delivery guy. What unites them is this reverence for the culture of the open range and the things that make that life unique.

It's a place where different cultures find common ground. Florida Crackers, Montana cow folks, Mexican Rancheros, and simple "Yellowstone" fans who've never so much as pet a horse, never mind sat one.

I've found people to be polite and generous. I was at Cheyenne a few years ago and was waiting in the ticket line. I struck up a conversation with the lady in front of me. After a while she said she had an extra ticket she wasn't going to use and just gave it to me. Row 3 behind the bull chutes. That's a pretty big deal. Another time I was a dollar short at the hotdog stand (and didn't feel like breaking a $100). It was closing, end of the event. I was trying to get the kid to understand that at that point it didn't matter, they're tossing the remainder into the trash. After a moment another kid who had already gotten hers swung back and gave them the dollar for me.

It's little things like that but hang around long enough and you'll notice.

CIRCLE B
IRRIGATION

HERITAGE
AUTO

Priefer
THESE COLORS
DON'T RUN

American
WSM
auctioneers
DAKOTA RODEO
COMPANY
PEAKINS, OK - MANDAN, ND

Last thoughts on Rodeo, Ranching, and ReGenerative Agriculture

Rodeo has its roots in the business of raising cattle for market. That, more than ever before, is under attack from many quarters. Forces ranging from climate activists to peddlers of lab grown proteins are coming after the ranching industry like never before. That's not to say there aren't some legitimate criticisms in all that. Corporate supply chains are not appealing things to behold, and the regular family run ranch is at the mercy of their ruthless enforcement of profit margins. It's not good for animals or people.

What is emerging, however, is that healthy rangelands are one of the most important things out there if you're concerned about the environment. The rates at which healthy grasslands cycle carbon, defeat heat sinks, and contribute to the water cycle far exceed forests. The health of that ecosystem is entirely dependent on ruminant animals who consume, digest, and discharge the digested grass and forbs as fertilizer, which they then till in with their hoofs. The even the climate folks at the UN and World Economic Forum admit this.

In centuries past this cycle was maintained in middle North America by Bison. Hence the super deep and fertile topsoil found on the Great Plains before it was subjected to industrial monocropping and mass chemical inputs. In some places the soil and root systems of the native grasses were 9ft deep. It was said on the plains of Nebraska in the mid-1800s that you could tie the heads of the grass across the horn of your saddle. Evolved to weather wet and dry cycles it was the height of grassland evolution. Population pressure and a subsequent priority on mass production, however, did immense damage to this.

So how do we get back to that state of ecological health and restore the natural cycles? ReGenerative agriculture practices that incorporate tightly managed, high density, rotational grazing, which mimics the pattern and impact of the Bison herds. Cattle is how that is going to happen. (I understand and support the efforts to reintroduce Bison. They are not, however, going to replace cattle in the human food chain and if this is going to work, that's going to have to be part of the paradigm. That's just the reality of it.)

So, we're back to ranching and running cows, and by extension the skill sets and culture that embodies rodeo.

Made in United States
North Haven, CT
05 November 2023

43660872R00049